MAY 2017

Bo Loves
to Row

Jan Westberg

Consulting Editor, Diane Craig, M.A./Reading Specialist

ABDO
Publishing Company

Published by ABDO Publishing Company, 4940 Viking Drive, Edina, Minnesota 55435.

Printed in the United States.

Credits
Edited by: Pam Price
Curriculum Coordinator: Nancy Tuminelly
Cover and Interior Design and Production: Mighty Media
Photo and Illustration Credits: BananaStock Ltd., Brand X Pictures, Eyewire Images, Hemera, Image 100, Image Source, Tracy Kompelien, PhotoDisc, Stockbyte, Thinkstock

Library of Congress Cataloging-in-Publication Data

Westberg, Jan.
    Bo loves to row / Jan Westberg.
        p. cm. -- (Rhyme time)
    Includes index.
    ISBN 1-59197-777-0 (hardcover)
    ISBN 1-59197-883-1 (paperback)
    1. English language--Rhyme--Juvenile literature. I. Title. II. Rhyme time (ABDO Publishing Company)

PE1517.W474 2004
428.1'3--dc22
                                                                        2004050798

SandCastle™ books are created by a professional team of educators, reading specialists, and content developers around five essential components that include phonemic awareness, phonics, vocabulary, text comprehension, and fluency. All books are written, reviewed, and leveled for guided reading, early intervention reading, and Accelerated Reader® programs and designed for use in shared, guided, and independent reading and writing activities to support a balanced approach to literacy instruction.

Let Us Know

After reading the book, SandCastle would like you to tell us your stories about reading. What is your favorite page? Was there something hard that you needed help with? Share the ups and downs of learning to read. We want to hear from you! To get posted on the ABDO Publishing Company Web site, send us e-mail at:

sandcastle@abdopub.com

SandCastle Level: Transitional

Words that rhyme do not have to be spelled the same. These words rhyme with each other:

ago

low

blow

no

flow

row

go

so

hello

tow

If you want to inflate a balloon, you have to **blow**.

Nell is eight years old today.

She turned seven a year **ago**.

Colby and John like to sit by the creek and watch the water **flow**.

Trisha, Marc, and their friends are running as fast as they can go.

When you go down a slide, you start out high and end up **low**.

When Ron gets home from school, his father is waiting to say **hello**.

These students are sitting in a row.

When Carlos asks Loni if he can have her carrots, she says no!

Harry isn't very heavy, so he is easy to **tow**.

Grace works hard on her essay **so** she will get a good grade.

Bo Loves to Row

Above the sea,
on a high plateau,
there was a tiny
bungalow.

15

Living there was a man named Bo.
He loved to take his boat and row.

One evening
not so long ago,
the tide was very low.

Bo saw a whale
far below.

The poor whale was stuck
and could not blow.

Bo thought, "Oh no!
That poor whale needs a tow."
Bo was not slow
and got ready to go.

19

He got to the whale
and said, "Hello.

Have no fear, at this I'm a pro!"

So Bo began to row, and the water started to flow.

The happy whale let out a great big blow!

What do you call a
greeting spoken with a deep voice?

Low hello

Glossary

bungalow. a small house or cottage

creek. a small, shallow stream that often flows to a river

inflate. to fill with air or another gas

plateau. A flat area of land that is raised above the surrounding land

tide. the rise and fall of the surface of the ocean and the bays and inlets connected to it

tow. to pull or drag something behind you

About SandCastle™

A professional team of educators, reading specialists, and content developers created the SandCastle™ series to support young readers as they develop reading skills and strategies and increase their general knowledge. The SandCastle™ series has four levels that correspond to early literacy development in young children. The levels are provided to help teachers and parents select the appropriate books for young readers.

Emerging Readers
(no flags)

Beginning Readers
(1 flag)

Transitional Readers
(2 flags)

Fluent Readers
(3 flags)

These levels are meant only as a guide. All levels are subject to change.

ABDO
Publishing Company

To see a complete list of SandCastle™ books and other nonfiction titles from ABDO Publishing Company, visit www.abdopub.com or contact us at: 4940 Viking Drive, Edina, Minnesota 55435 • 1-800-800-1312 • fax: 1-952-831-1632